Smart Word Tracing For Children

by Elite Schooler Workbooks

Important Legal Information:

This workbook contains reproducibles. These are worksheets designed with the goal of being photocopied as much as required. Accordingly, I grant you the non-commercial right to photocopy any part of this workbook for any non-commercial, or educational, use.

All further rights are reserved © 2019.

ISBN: 9781704001562

Dolch Second Grade Sight Words

Always always	Does does	Made made	Tell tell	Why why
Around around	Don't don't	Many many	Their their	Wish wish
Because because	Fast fast	Off off	These these	Work work
Been been	First first	Or or	Those those	Would would
Before before	Five five	Pull pull	Upon upon	Write write
Best best	Found found	Read read	Us us	Your your
Both both	Gave gave	Right right	Use use	
Buy buy	Goes goes	Sing sing	Very very	
Call call	Green green	Sit sit	Wash wash	
Cold cold	Its its	Sleep sleep	Which which	

Instructions For The Educator

Trace from the circle...
...to the tip of the arrow
Numbers give you a suggested stroke order
Remember: Strokes are only numbered when a letter is drawn with two or more strokes.

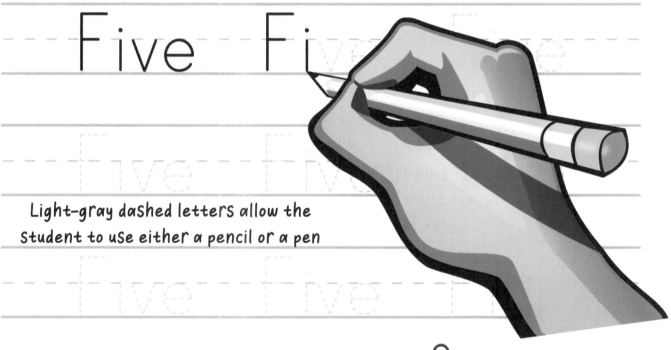

Light-gray dashed letters allow the student to use either a pencil or a pen

The remaining empty rows provide room for free practice, allowing you to evaluate student progress

Remember: Empty worksheets at the end of your workbook offer ample extra room for free practice.

How To Use The Empty Worksheets

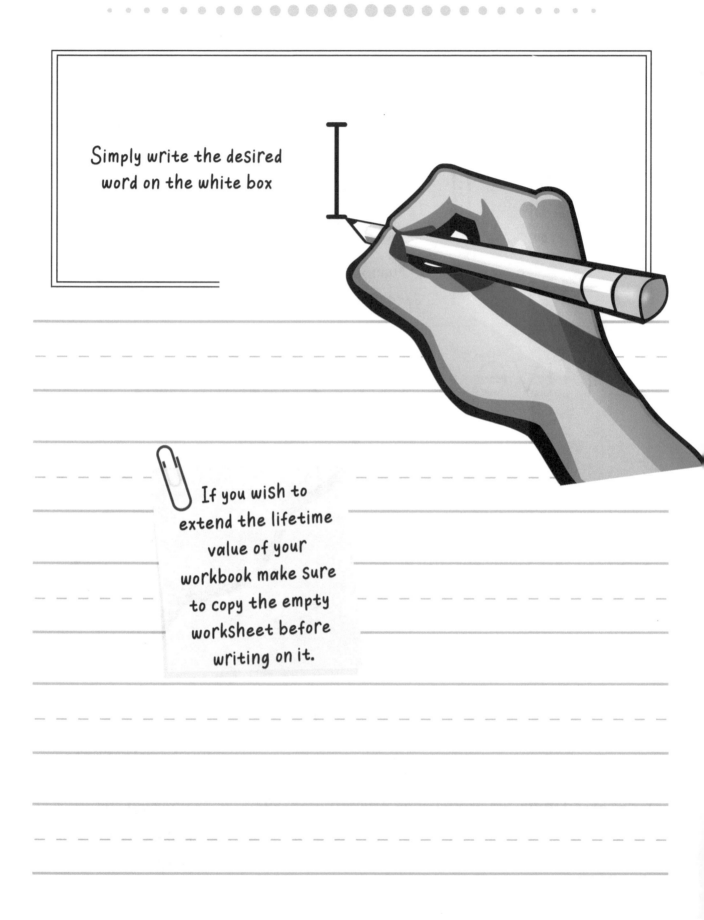

Simply write the desired word on the white box

If you wish to extend the lifetime value of your workbook make sure to copy the empty worksheet before writing on it.

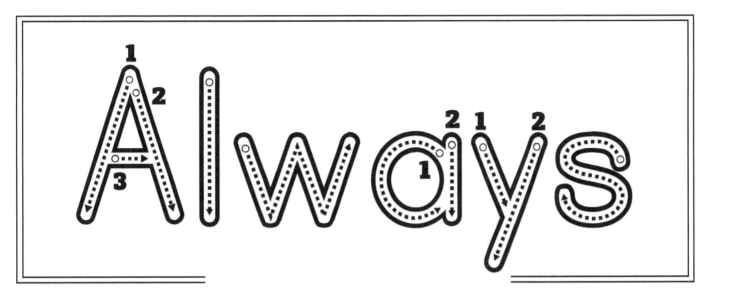

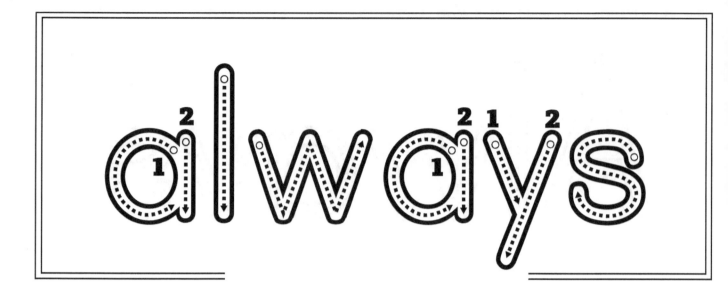

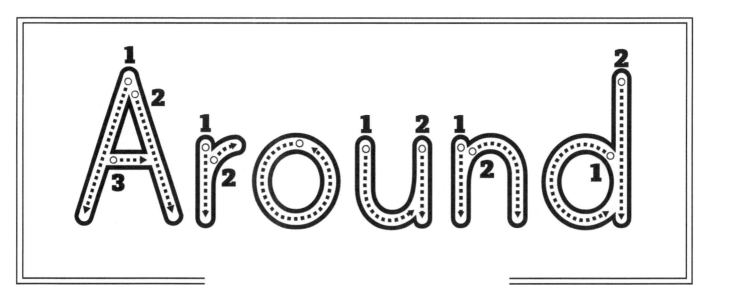

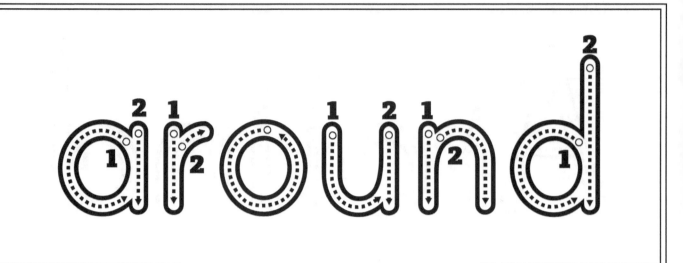

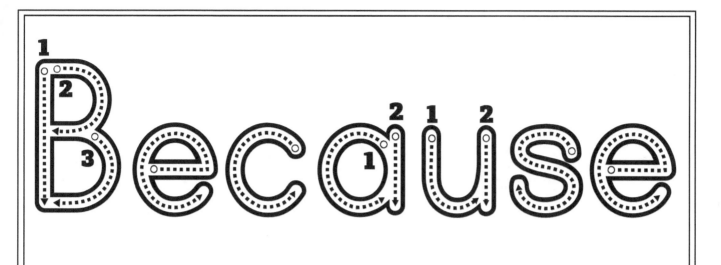

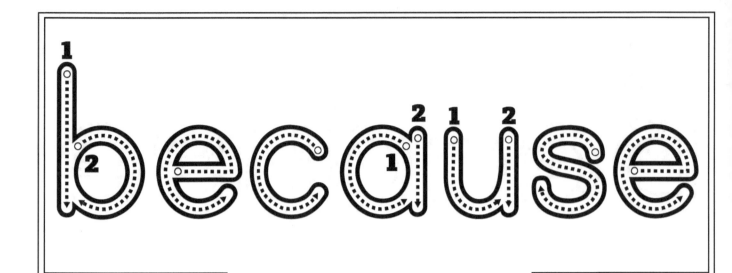

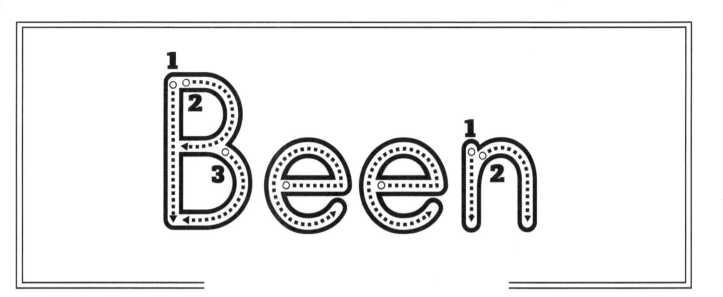

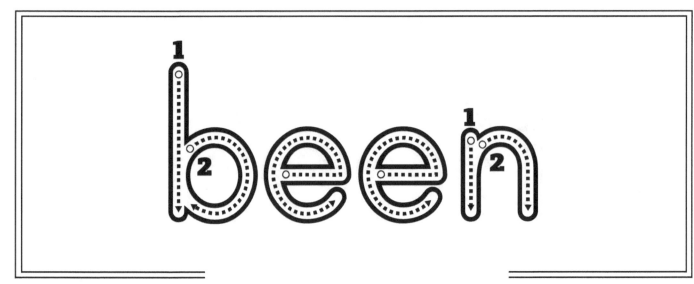

been   been   been

been   been   been

been   been   been

Before

Before   Before

Before   Before

Before   Before

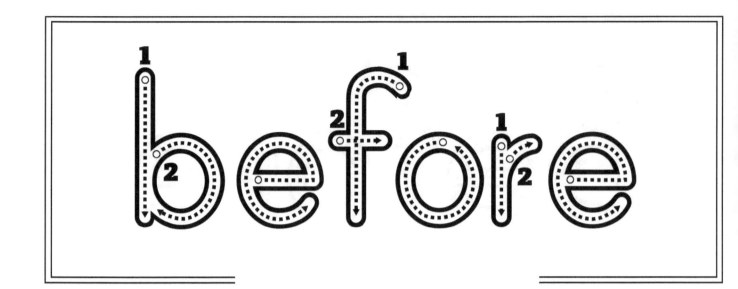

before   before

before   before

before   before

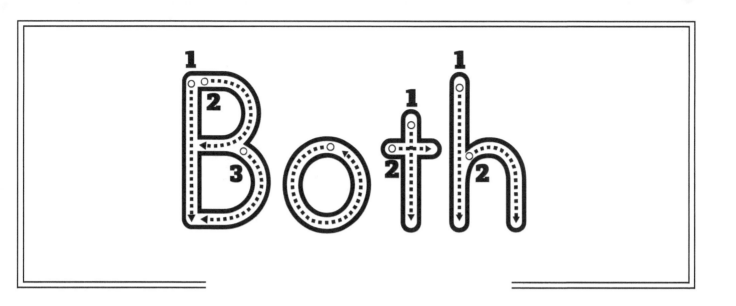

Both Both Both

Both Both Both

Both Both Both

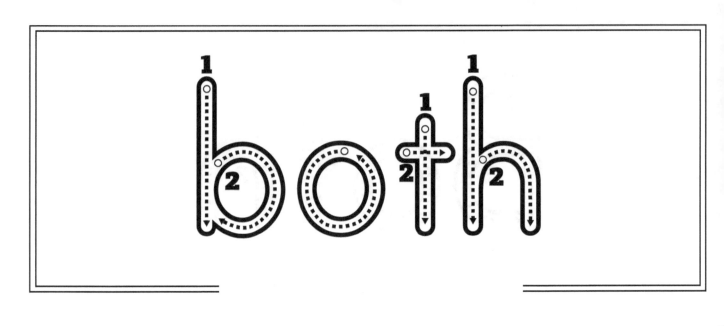

both both both

both both both

both both both

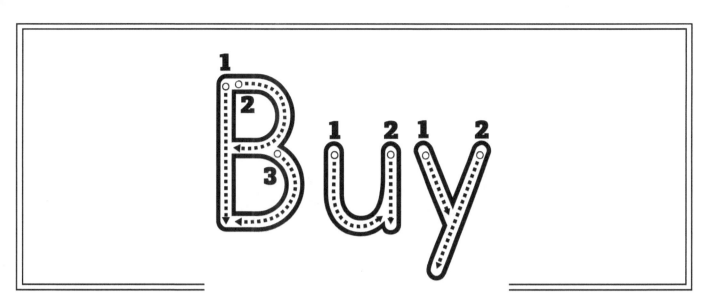

Buy   Buy   Buy   Buy

Buy   Buy   Buy   Buy

Buy   Buy   Buy   Buy

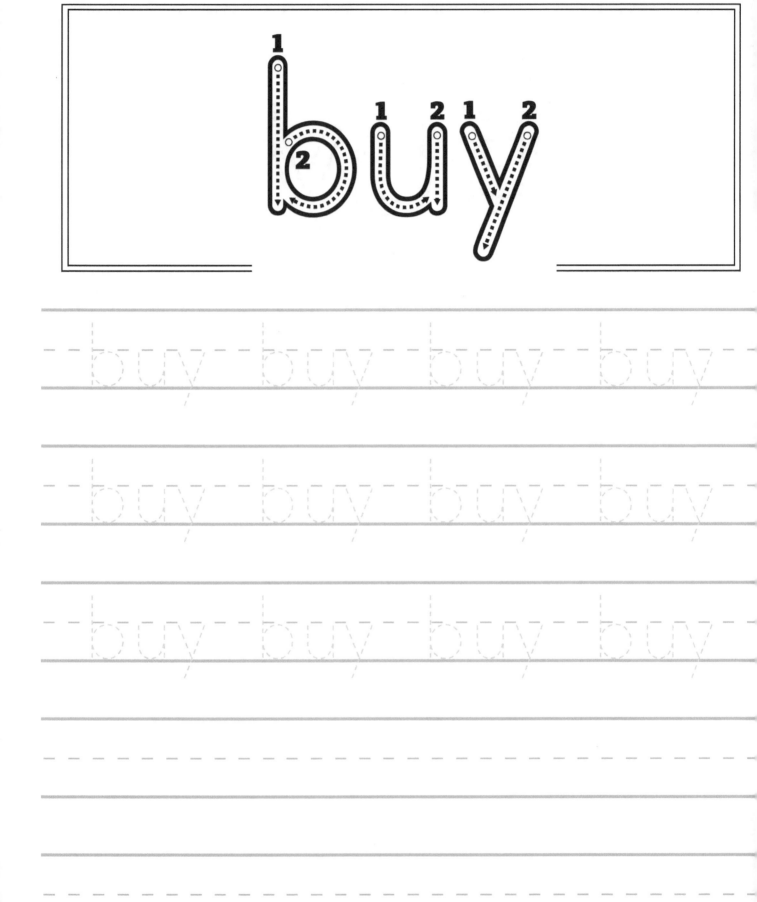

Call

Call Call Call Call

Call Call Call Call

Call Call Call Call

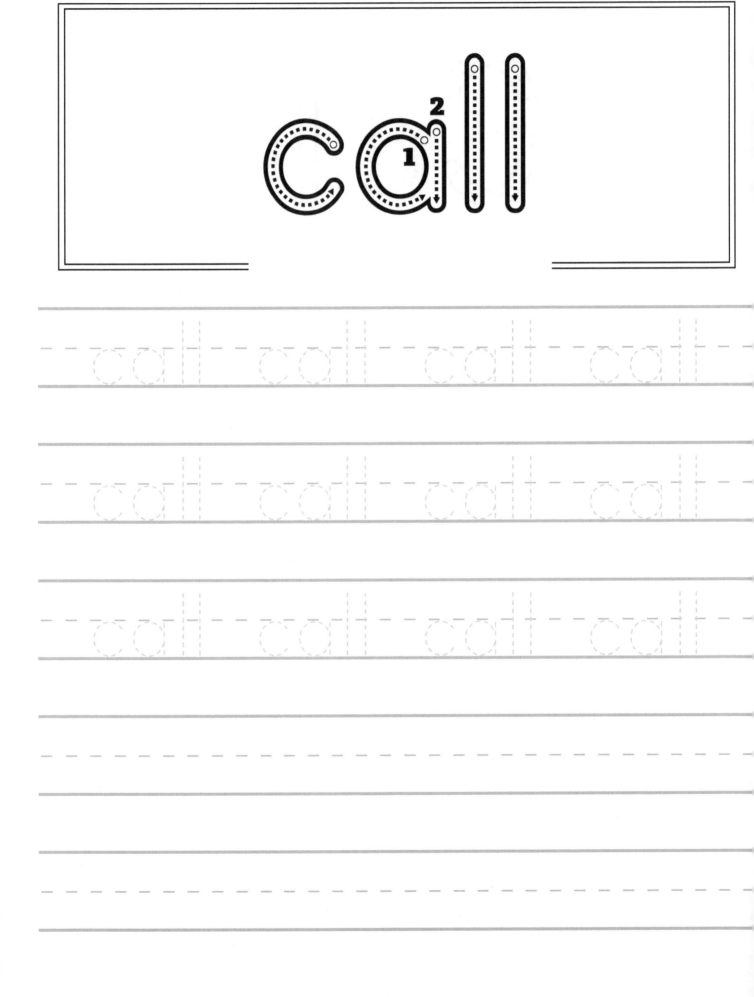

Cold

Cold   Cold   Cold

Cold   Cold   Cold

Cold   Cold   Cold

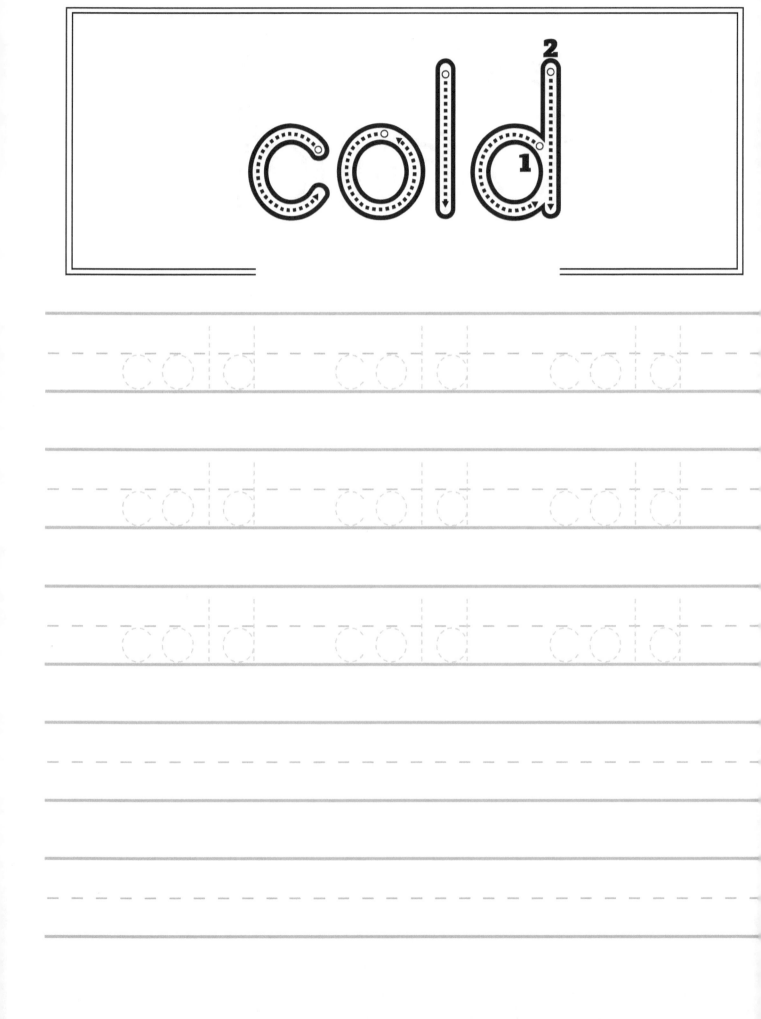

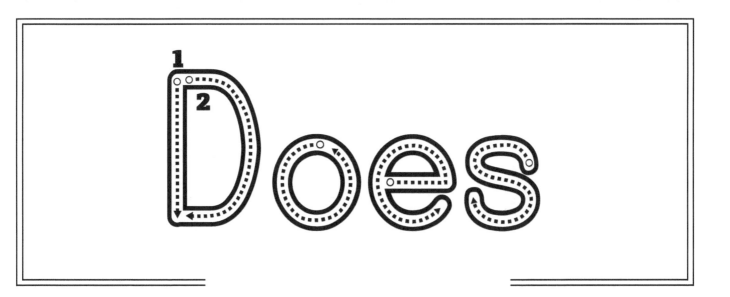

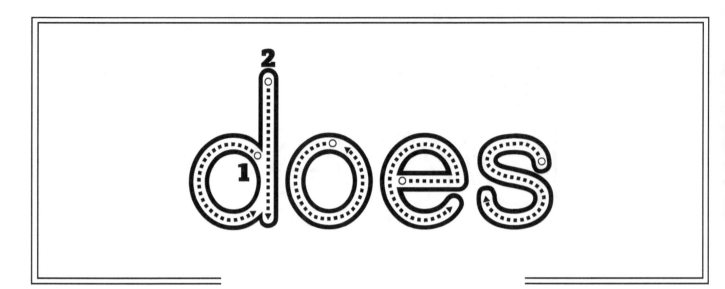

does does does

does does does

does does does

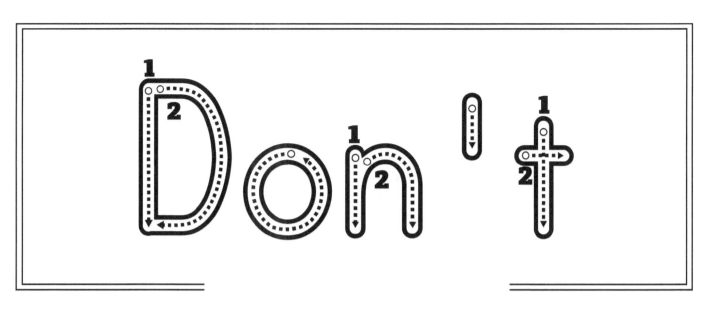

Don't   Don't   Don't

Don't   Don't   Don't

Don't   Don't   Don't

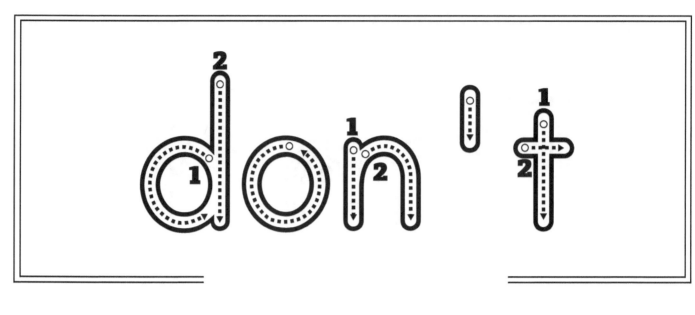

don't   don't   don't

don't   don't   don't

don't   don't   don't

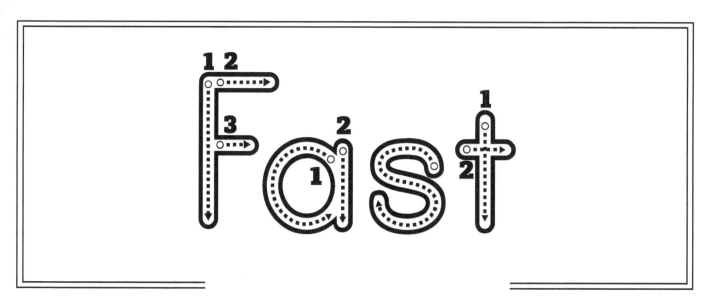

fast   fast   fast

fast   fast   fast

fast   fast   fast

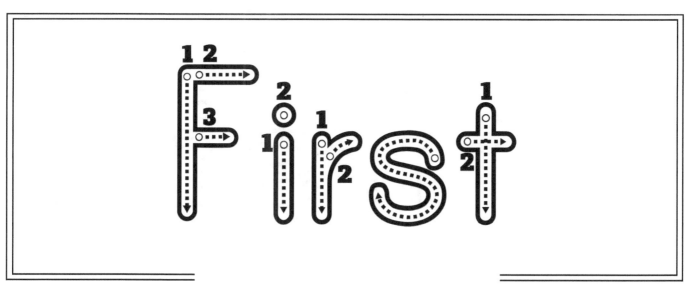

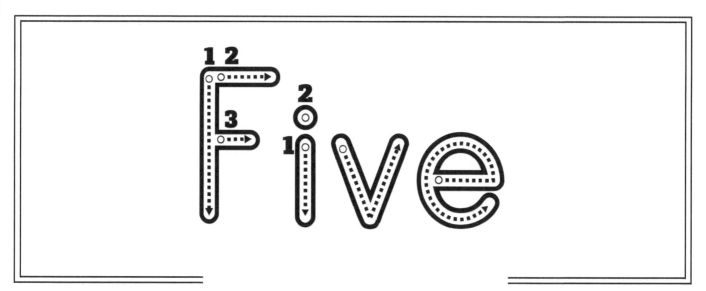

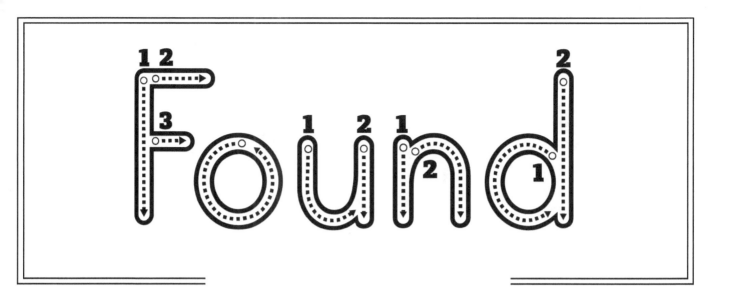

found found

found found

found found

Gave

Gave Gave Gave

Gave Gave Gave

Gave Gave Gave

Goes

Goes   Goes   Goes

Goes   Goes   Goes

Goes   Goes   Goes

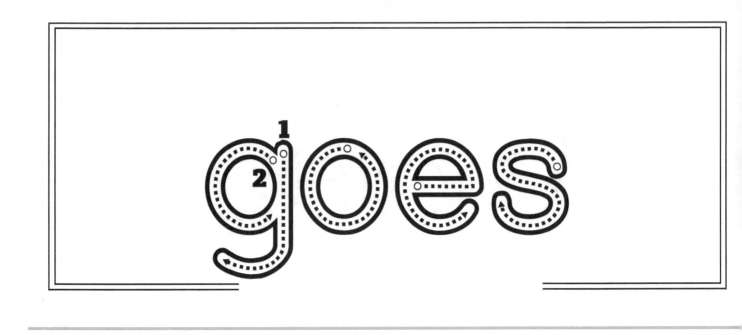

goes   goes   goes

goes   goes   goes

goes   goes   goes

Green   Green

Green   Green

Green   Green

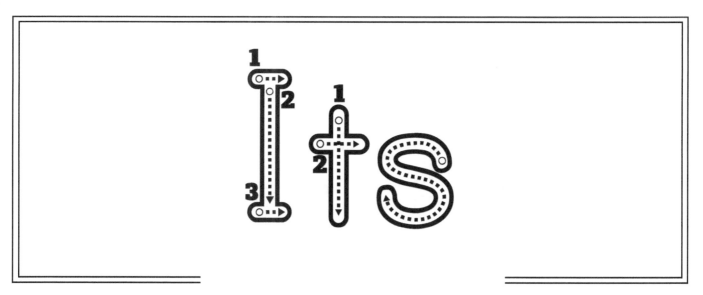

Its Its Its Its

Its Its Its Its

Its Its Its Its

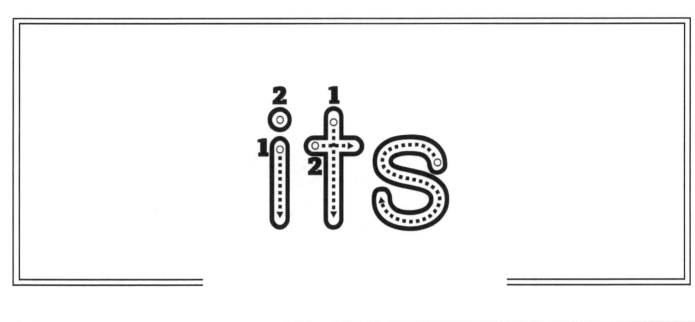

its its its its its

its its its its its

its its its its its

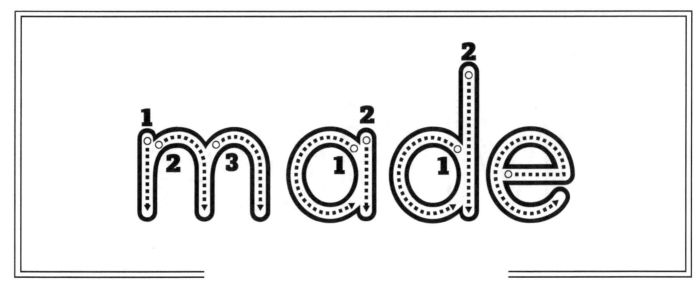

Many

Many Many Many

Many Many Many

Many Many Many

many many many

many many many

many many many

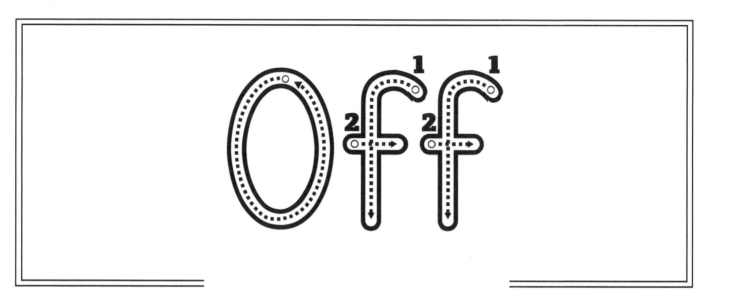

off off off off

off off off off

off off off off

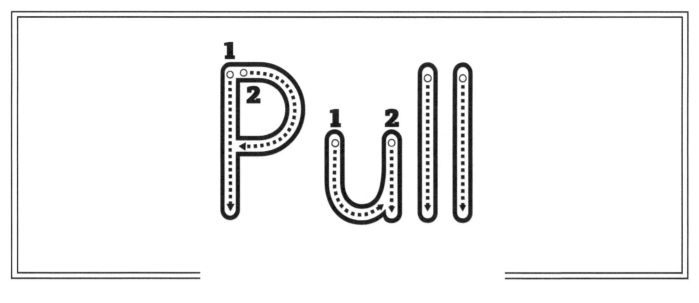

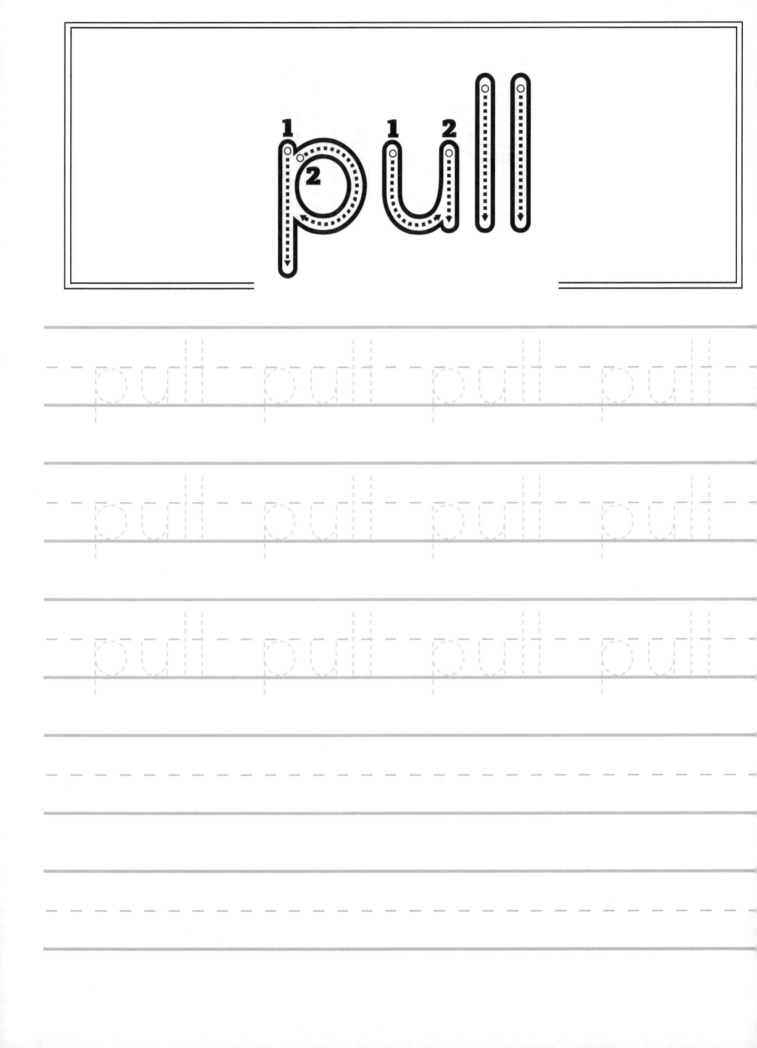

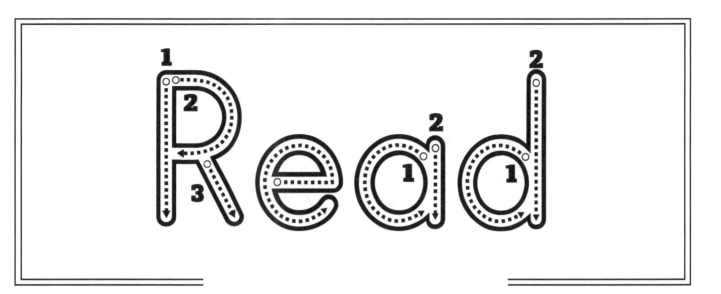

Read   Read   Read

Read   Read   Read

Read   Read   Read

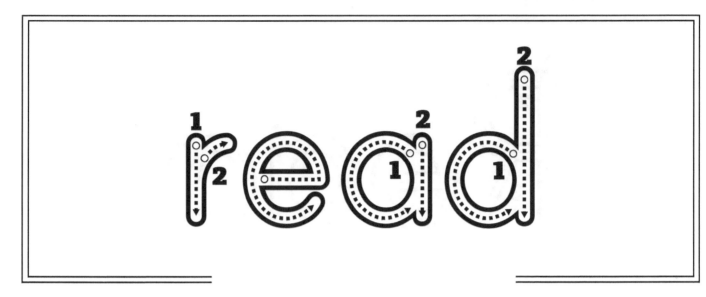

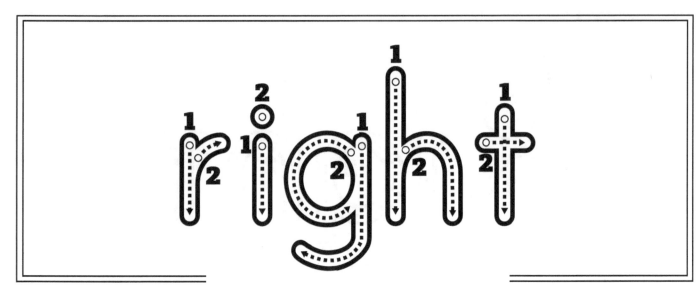

Sing

Sing   Sing   Sing

Sing   Sing   Sing

Sing   Sing   Sing

Sit

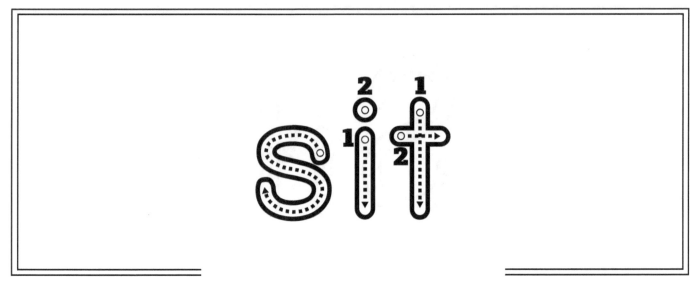

Sleep

Sleep   Sleep   Sleep

Sleep   Sleep   Sleep

Sleep   Sleep   Sleep

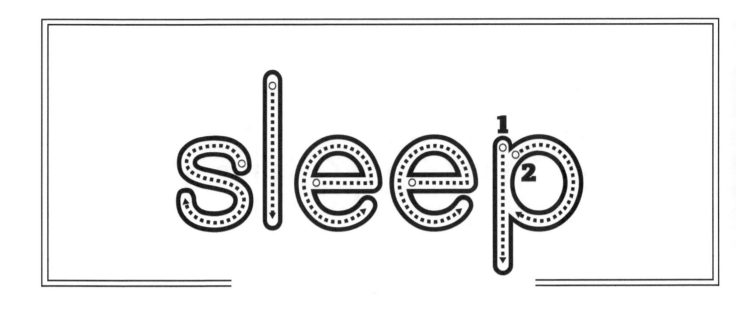

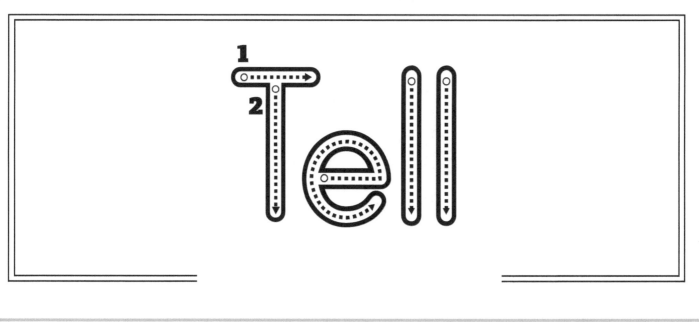

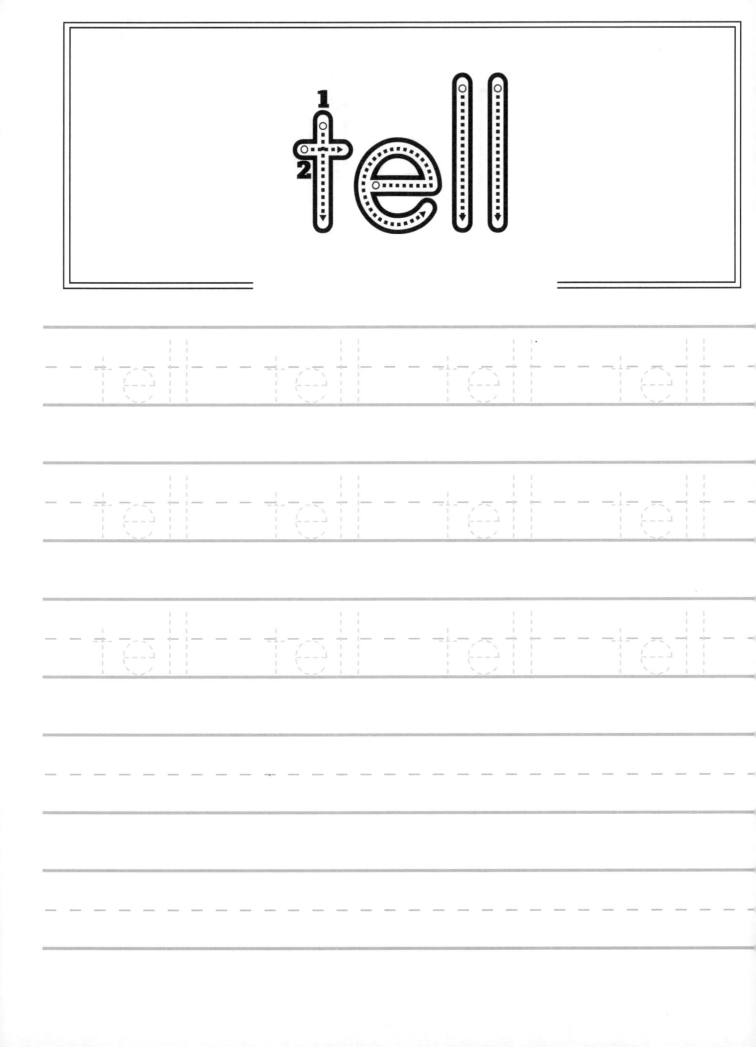

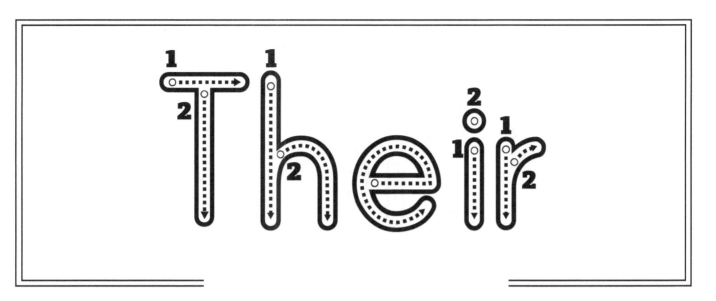

Their Their Their

Their Their Their

Their Their Their

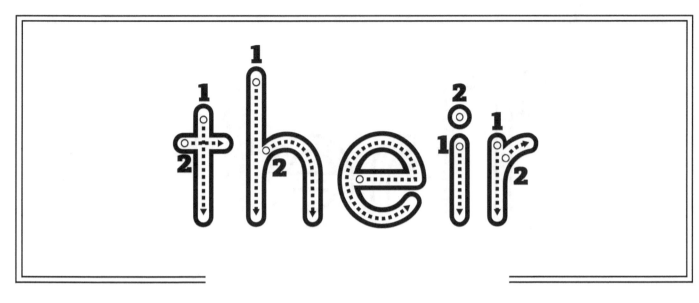

their their their

their their their

their their their

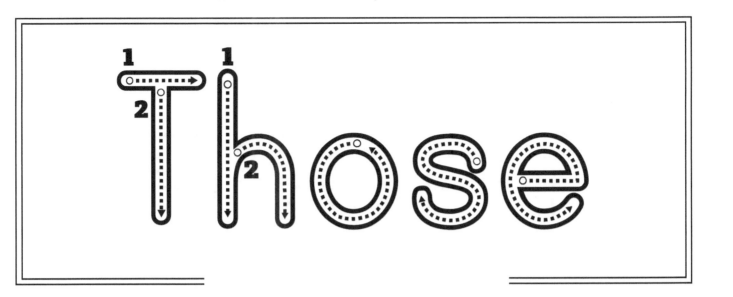

Those   Those

Those   Those

Those   Those

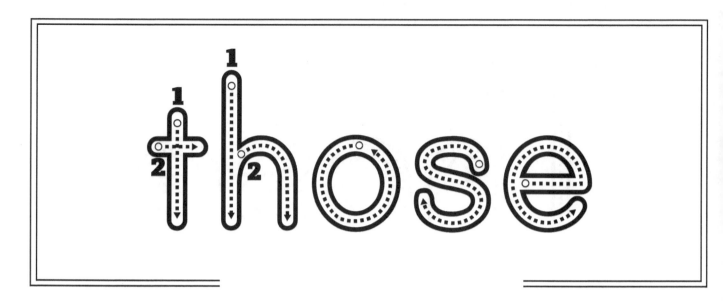

those those

those those

those those

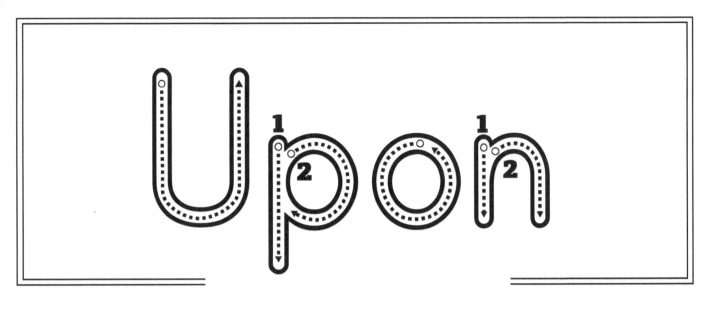

Upon Upon Upon

Upon Upon Upon

Upon Upon Upon

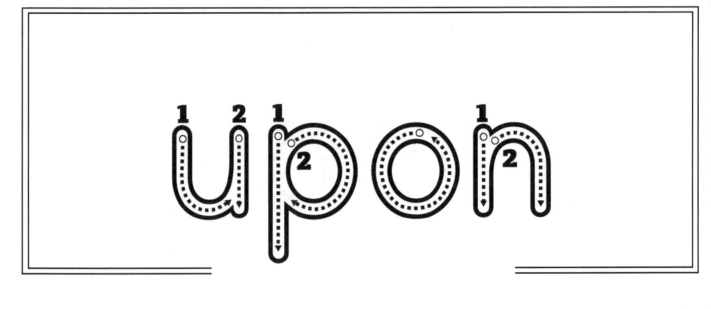

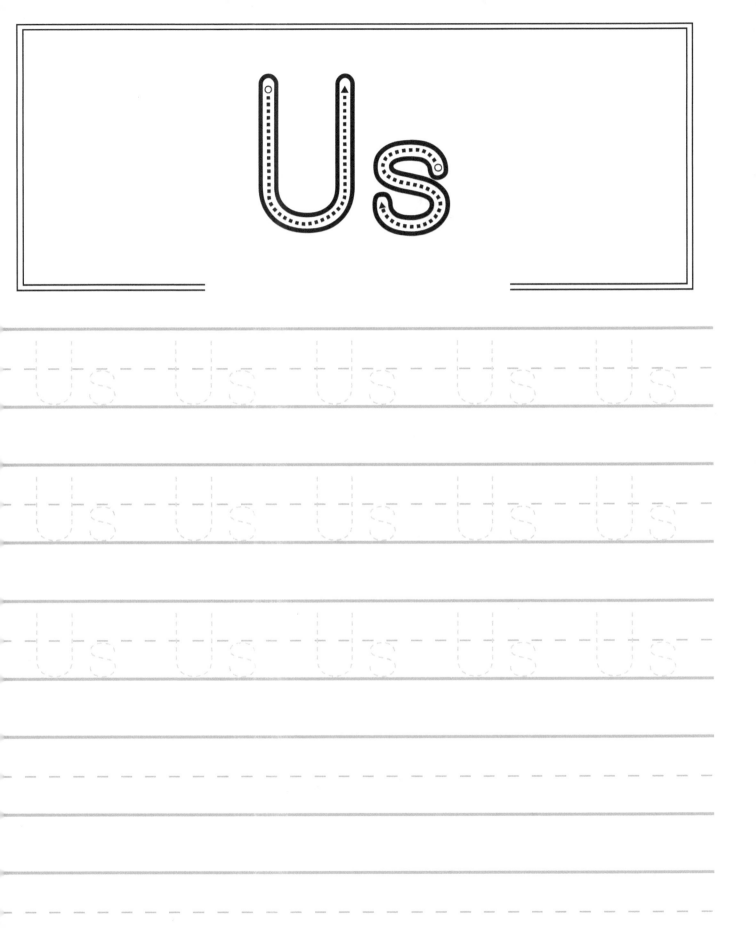

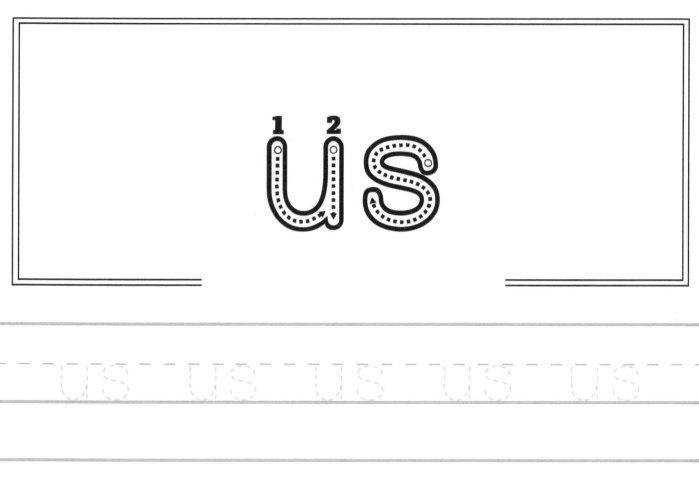

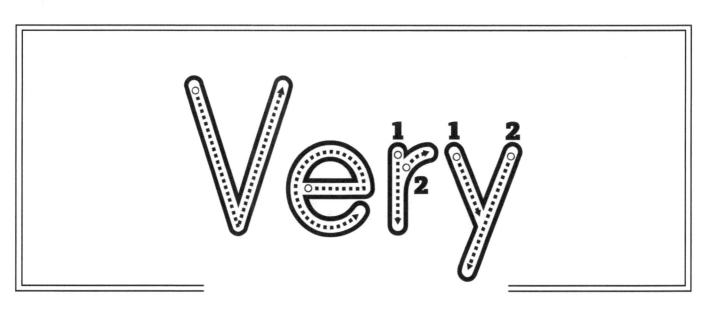

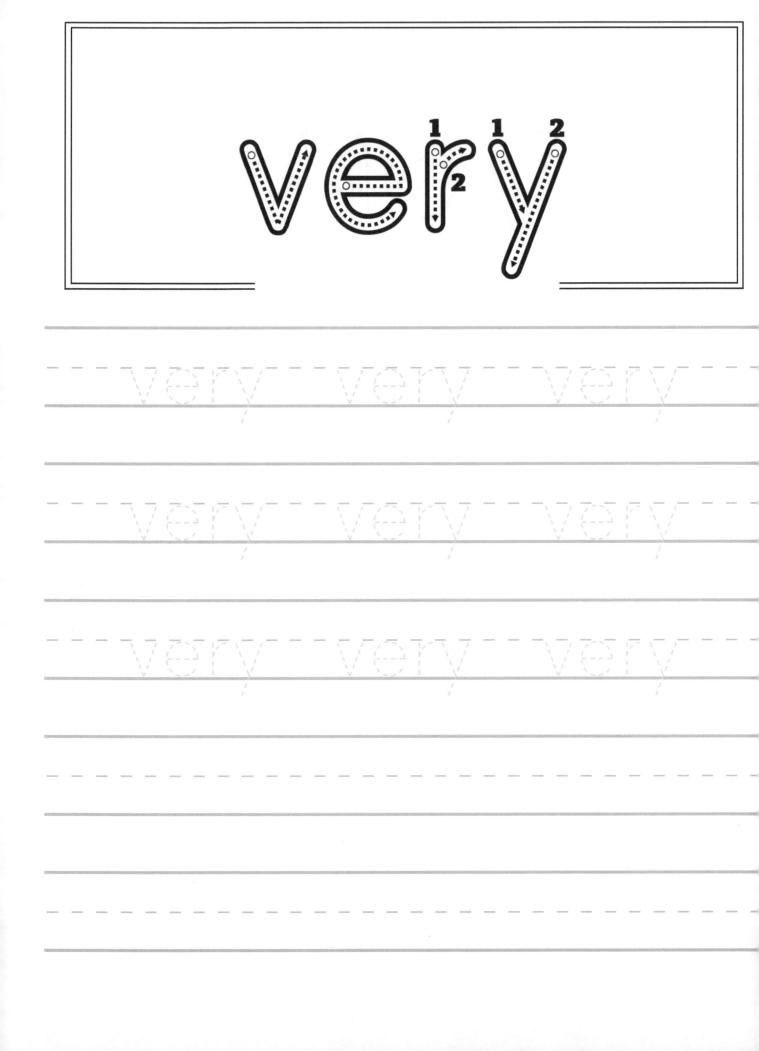

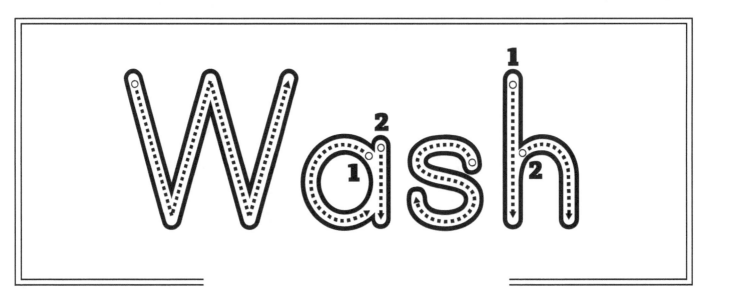

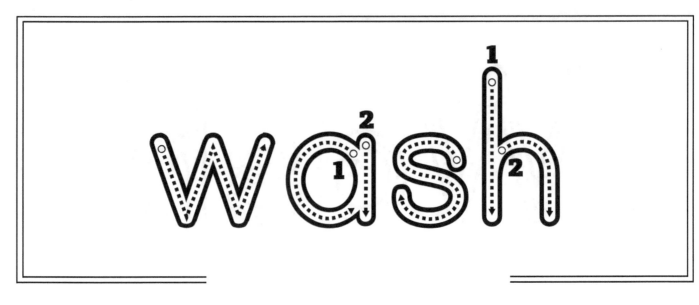

wash wash wash

wash wash wash

wash wash wash

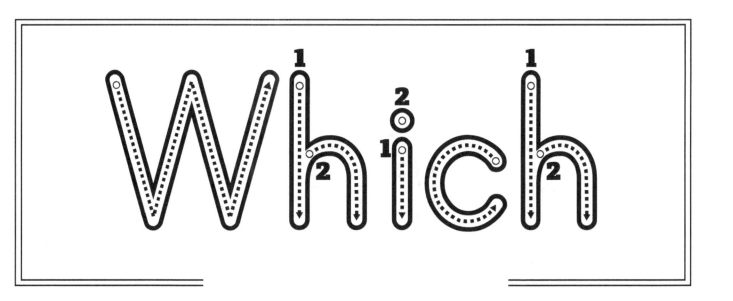

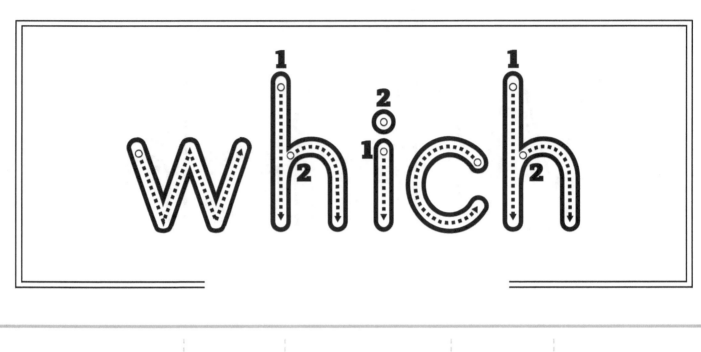

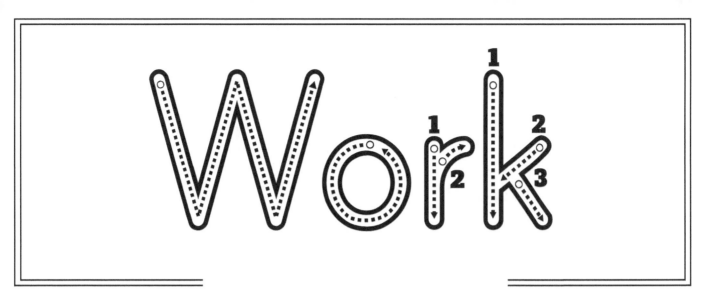

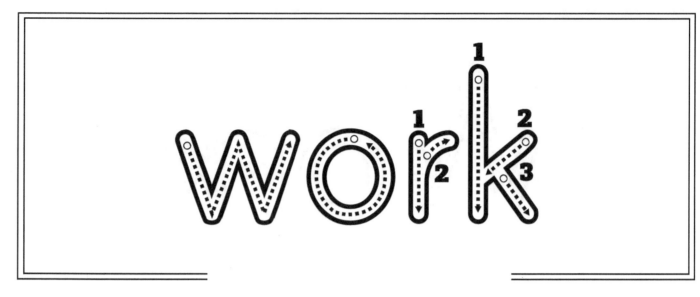

work work work

work work work

work work work

Would

Would   Would

Would   Would

Would   Would

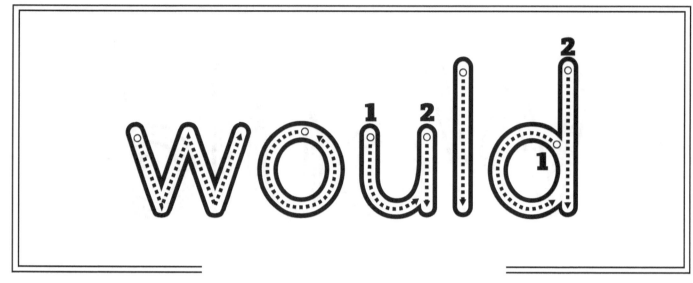

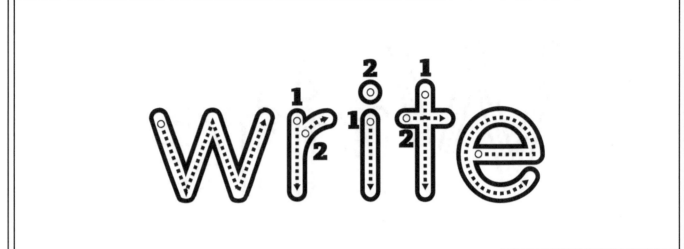

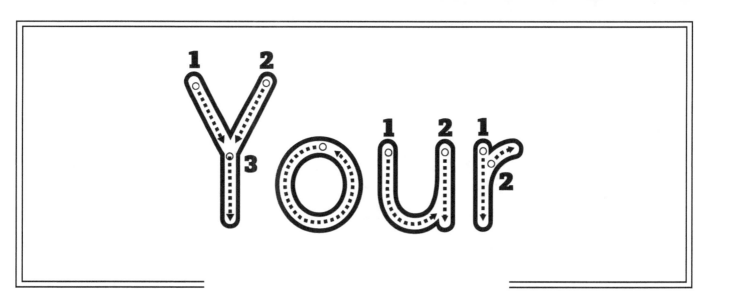

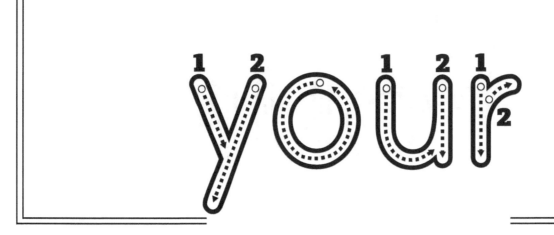

your   your   your

your   your   your

your   your   your

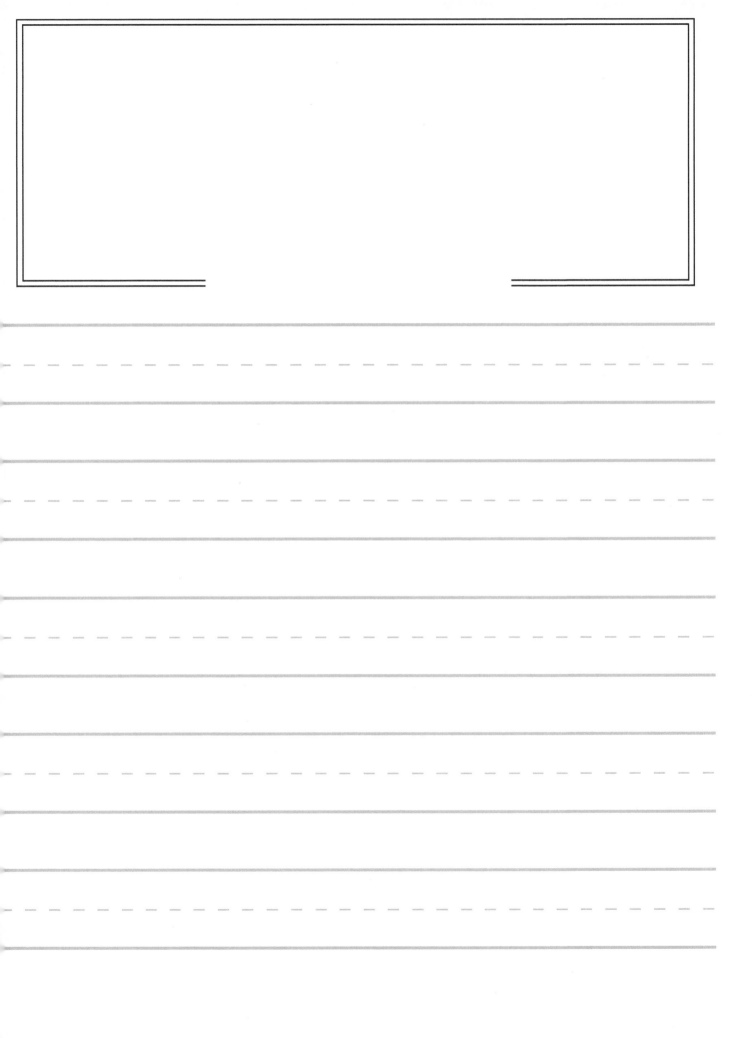

Made in United States
Troutdale, OR
05/09/2024